AUDIO ACCESS INCLUDED

EXTREME METAL BASS

ESSENTIAL TECHNIQUES, CONCEPTS, AND APPLICATIONS FOR METAL BASSISTS

BY ALEX WEBSTER of CANNIBAL CORPSE

PLAYBACK+
Speed • Pitch • Balance • Loop

To access audio visit:
www.halleonard.com/mylibrary

Enter Code
5102-9198-3607-9385

All photos by Alison Webster

ISBN 978-1-4234-9715-8

HAL•LEONARD®
CORPORATION
7777 W. BLUEMOUND RD. P.O. BOX 13819 MILWAUKEE, WI 53213

In Australia Contact:
Hal Leonard Australia Pty. Ltd.
4 Lentara Court
Cheltenham, Victoria, 3192 Australia
Email: ausadmin@halleonard.com.au

Visit Hal Leonard Online at
www.halleonard.com

CONTENTS

INTRODUCTION

Hello and welcome to *Extreme Metal Bass*. The goal of this book is to help you learn the bass guitar techniques commonly used in modern extreme metal and to show you how these techniques are applied within the context of a song.

When I began playing bass in the mid eighties, I wasn't able to find any instructional material that applied directly to extreme metal. Sure, there were a lot of useful books and videos available about general bass playing, but nothing focused on the more aggressive forms of heavy metal. Even now, more than two decades later, there's still very little material available in this area. With this book, I will attempt to change that by sharing some of the things I've learned throughout my career as a bassist in one of the world's top death metal bands.

The lack of instructional material available at the time I started playing bass wasn't that surprising, since extreme metal had only been around for a few years (thrash, death, and black metal were still in their earliest stages of development in the mid eighties). The genre was not established enough to have generated standards and rules that its musicians were expected to follow. I think the absence of rules was actually a good thing; it forced us to be creative, rather than rely on what came before us.

In this freewheeling musical environment, the players on the scene used trial and error to figure out what sounded best. For example, there was no precedent for what a bassist should play during a speed-picked guitar part, so each player had to figure out his own way of doing things in that situation (my solutions to this particular musical problem are detailed in Chapter 8). Some of the most interesting musical ideas have probably been invented by musicians who didn't know what the "right" thing to play was!

So, with this in mind, remember that the techniques and concepts presented in this book are not intended to be rules, but rather a selection of things I've found that work for me and may also work for you. After you learn them, I would encourage you to build upon them by adding your own ideas. If you develop your own techniques and concepts by adapting mine (or, even better, invent something entirely new), that's fantastic and completely in keeping with the "no rules" spirit that helped give rise to this form of music. Learning the rules of music can be very helpful, but you should never be afraid to break those rules.

Work through all of the chapters in order. By the end of this book, you will be able to handle many of the musical situations you'll encounter in extreme metal. If you do encounter something not covered in this book, hopefully the concepts for bass line creation discussed in these pages will spur your creativity and help you find a new musical solution. When that happens, you will have added a little something to the musical lexicon of extreme metal, and that is something to be proud of. Extreme metal still is a relatively new form of music; therefore, we all can participate in its development. Seize the opportunity and leave your mark!

NOTES

A WORD ABOUT THE TITLE

The title of this book is *Extreme Metal Bass*. I felt that title was appropriate since the label "extreme metal" generally is used as an umbrella term that includes all of the more intense forms of heavy metal: thrash, death, black, metalcore, deathcore, etc. Basically, any form of heavy metal that is more likely to inspire slam dancing than fist banging probably could be considered extreme metal.

I have tried to create exercises that will improve your bass playing skills, regardless of which sub-genre of extreme metal you have chosen to play. Throughout the book, you'll find exercises that might remind you of one sub-genre or another. I advise you to learn all of the exercises, even if you think they might not apply directly to your particular sub-genre. The wide variety of exercises presented within these pages are designed to prepare you for whatever challenges you'll face as an extreme metal bassist. I felt that focusing narrowly on one sub-genre or another would be too limiting. Also, I think you'll find that most of the techniques used in one style of extreme metal do apply to the others. For example, if you master a speed-picking technique in a thrash metal example, that same technique also is often used in death, black, and other extreme metal forms. So, although the exercises in this book may not always be written in your favorite style of extreme metal, the skills you develop by practicing them will help you become a better bassist, regardless of the style.

HOW TO USE THIS BOOK

This book is designed for players who use a standard-tuned five-string bass (low to high: B–E–A–D–G). If you do not have a five-string bass, a four-string (tuned B–E–A–D) will work for much of the material presented.

Throughout this book, I will be referring to the fret hand as the "left" hand and the plucking hand as the "right" hand, since a majority of people are right-handed. Obviously, if you're a lefty, just reverse these references.

Since I'm strictly a fingerstyle player, I decided that I would not attempt to cover any pick (plectrum) techniques within these pages. I never play with a pick, so I certainly wouldn't try to teach someone else how to use one! That said, I think bassists who play with a pick can get a lot of use out of this book. In fact, even if you prefer fingerstyle, you might find that a pick works better for you on certain exercises. Experiment and find the combination of techniques that suits you best.

ABOUT THE AUDIO

The audio that accompanies this book features play-along tracks for all of the examples shown in the "Application" section of the book (Chapters 5 through 10). Both full band and guitar/drums-only versions of each example are included.

I also have included MIDI files of the drum patterns for these exercises. Since many musicians these days have easy access to a digital audio workstation (DAW) like Pro Tools, Garageband, Cubase, etc., I thought that making these files available could be very helpful for practicing. Using your computer, you can easily import the MIDI files from Hal Leonard's My Library to your DAW of choice and assign drum sounds. Since it's extremely easy to switch tempos in most DAWs, you'll be able to practice with the drum tracks playing back as slowly or rapidly as you like. This can be very helpful when learning tricky sections of songs.

Tuning notes can be found on Track 1.

Track 1

THE RHYTHM SECTION IN EXTREME METAL

The term "rhythm section" generally refers to the members of a musical group that create the rhythmic pulse of the song. In extreme metal, there are a few different approaches to the rhythm section; I will briefly describe three of the most common.

Traditional Drum/Bass

The first approach is what I refer to as the "traditional drum/bass" rhythm section. In this approach, the bass line closely follows the kick and snare patterns played by the drummer, often playing a line that is quite different from the rhythm guitar riff. This approach is extremely common in traditional heavy metal and hard rock, though occasionally it can be heard in modern extreme metal as well. Bob Daisley's staccato, kick/snare-based bass lines on the Ozzy Osbourne songs "Crazy Train" and "I Don't Know" are great examples of this approach.

Guitar/Bass

The second approach is one that became common with the advent of thrash metal. In this approach, the bass locks in with the rhythm guitar riff—rather than simply playing with the kick and snare—thereby creating a thicker sound. Thrash metal bassists like Cliff Burton (Metallica), Frank Bello (Anthrax), and D.D. Verni (Overkill) employed this approach, which I like to call the "guitar/bass" rhythm section. Check out D.D.'s playing on the Overkill song "Drunken Wisdom" to hear a great example of a guitar/bass rhythm section—just one of many such great examples to be found in eighties thrash.

Guitar/Bass/Kick Drum

The third approach we'll look at features the rhythm guitar, bass, and kick drum locking in to the same rhythm. Essentially, this is a combination of the first two approaches—all three instruments play together to form one big rhythm section. I've nicknamed it the "bulldozer of rhythm" because the musical effect is reminiscent of heavy machinery. Early on, this approach was most often heard as a straight double-kick pattern that followed a straight guitar/bass line, but as it evolved, you started to hear it being applied to more complex rhythms. For a great example of how this approach is applied in modern extreme metal, listen to Meshuggah bassist Dick Lövgren lock in with the rhythm guitar and kick drum patterns in the song "Bleed."

These three rhythm section approaches can be found throughout this book. For specific examples, check out these:

- Traditional drum/bass pattern: First half of Example 7-2
- Guitar/bass pattern: Example 6-1
- Guitar/bass/kick-drum patterns: All of the exercises in Chapter 5

Once you become comfortable with these approaches, try using various combinations of them in your own music. By utilizing multiple rhythm section approaches in your songs, you can make your band sound much more dynamic than if you stuck to only one.

NOTES ON PRACTICING

Practice everything slowly at first, preferably using a metronome, drum machine, or (if you have access to a DAW) the included MIDI drum tracks. I think you'll be amazed at how much your ability to play fast will improve if you take the time to first practice slowly.

Try recording yourself playing along with the guitar/drums-only tracks. After you've recorded, listen closely for timing issues, weakly played notes, extra string noise, and other inconsistencies. It's better to isolate and correct flaws in your playing at home than have them pointed out to you by an engineer in the studio during a session. You can practice and eliminate your weak spots at home for free; studios charge by the hour!

Do not practice to the point of pain. This is extremely important and bears repeating, which I do a few times throughout this book. Learn to work with your hands' natural strengths and weaknesses and adjust accordingly. If you keep a sensible practice routine, your hands should become stronger and more flexible; you just need to be patient. Trying to make it happen overnight by over-practicing will more likely lead to injury than any improvement in your technique. Pace yourself, and don't overdo it!

Part 1: TECHNIQUE

CHAPTER 1:

IMPORTANT SCALES, INTERVALS, AND CHORDS FOR EXTREME METAL

While playing extreme metal, you are likely to encounter many riffs that have a dark and aggressive feeling to them. After all, that's the sort of vibe most extreme metal bands are going for. In Western music, all musicians have the same 12 notes to work with; it's the order and combination of these notes that give their music its character. If you're trying to create a dark, aggressive atmosphere with your music, learning the following scales, intervals, and chords will be very helpful.

SCALES

The following are a few scales that I have found very useful for creating riffs and bass lines in an extreme metal context. Of course, there are many other scales that can work well, too, but the ones shown here are a good starting point. The scales are shown here with an E root note.

I have included two fingerings for most of the scales. Be sure that you do not over-stretch your left hand while working on these patterns. Use the fingerings that are most comfortable for you. If you have small hands or are not that flexible, be wary of any patterns that require you to cover more than four frets with your left hand. "No pain, no gain" does NOT apply to practicing a musical instrument. Listen to your body's signals and avoid injury. Straining the tendons in your hand while trying to perform uncomfortable stretches will not make you a better bass player; after all, you can't practice while your hands are injured!

Natural Minor

This is the sixth mode of the major scale (Aeolian mode). It is most often heard in traditional and power metal.

Example 1-1:

Harmonic Minor

This scale is very useful for this type of music, perhaps even more so than the natural minor scale. The only difference between the two scales is that the 7th degree of the harmonic minor scale is raised a half step. This scale is often associated with the "neo-classical" sound in metal.

Example 1-2:

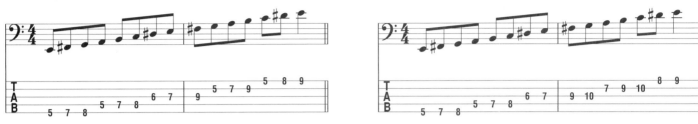

Hungarian Minor

This scale is similar to the harmonic minor scale but has been further altered by raising the 4th. This is arguably the darkest-sounding scale of the three minor scales I've shown here. This darker sound is produced, in part, by the raised 4th, which creates a tritone interval relative to the root note of the scale. The tritone is one of metal's most important intervals (see the interval section for more information).

Example 1-3:

Diminished 7th Arpeggio

As its name implies, this is not a scale but rather an *arpeggio* (a chord whose notes are played individually). I have included it in the scale section because it's an important part of several of these scales (look for it, starting from the 7th degree of the harmonic minor scale, as well as from *every* degree of the diminished scales). You will no doubt recognize this very familiar sound the moment you play it. The diminished 7th arpeggio is one of the most common patterns of notes in extreme metal.

Example 1-4:

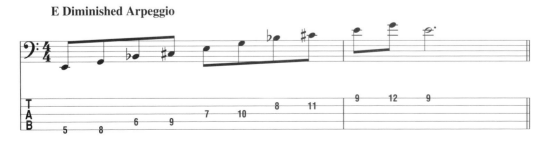

Diminished Scales

Diminished scales are built from either a whole step/half step pattern or a half step/whole step pattern. These scales are very useful for writing heavy riffs, as you will see in the pages that follow. As you become more familiar with these scales, you'll notice that there are really only three different diminished scales. For example, the E half/whole diminished scale contains the same eight notes as F whole/half diminished, G half/whole, A♭ whole/half, etc. F half/whole is the same scale as G♭ whole/half, etc. And F♯ half/whole is the same as G whole/half, and so on.

Example 1-5:

Minor Pentatonic

So named because of its five-tone structure, the pentatonic scale is extremely common in hard rock and early heavy metal. It can be useful in modern metal as well, though mainly for soloing and creating fills underneath power chords.

Example 1-6:

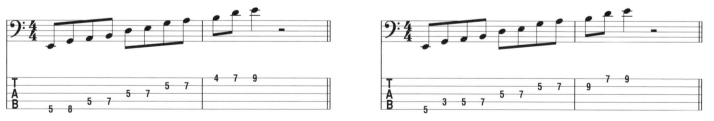

Blues Scale

The blues scale is a minor pentatonic scale with a tritone (a diminished 5th/augmented 4th) added. As with Hungarian minor, the tritone helps add a darker feeling to the scale. The blues scale is used in many of the same situations as the minor pentatonic scale.

Example 1-7:

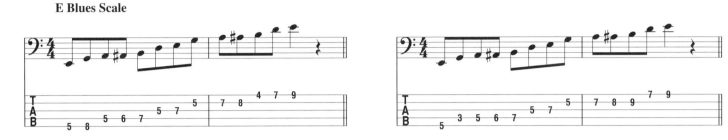

E Blues Scale

Whole-Tone Scale

Like the diminished scales, the whole-tone scale is composed of a symmetrical pattern of intervals; this time, it's entirely whole steps, as the name implies. There are only two different whole-tone scales. This scale is often considered to be more "weird" than "dark," but applied the right way, the whole-tone scale can be used to create some really interesting and heavy music.

Example 1-8:

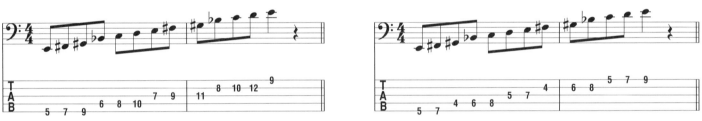

E Whole-Tone Scale

INTERVALS AND CHORDS

The distance between two notes is called an *interval*. Intervals are named for their size; that is, how far the pitches are located away from each other. For example, G is the third note in the E natural minor scale, so the interval from E to G is a minor 3rd. Other intervals are named in a similar way. For more information on the theory behind intervals and chords, I would recommend checking out a dedicated music theory book as a guide. Sean Malone's *Music Theory: A Practical, Easy to Use Guide for Bassists* (Hal Leonard) is an excellent choice.

The interval between notes can make a huge difference in the feeling those two notes produce. When an E is played with a G (a minor 3rd, as stated above), the result is a somber, darker feeling. When E is played with G♯ (a major 3rd), the result is a happier, more uplifting feeling. Since extreme metal music generally is not trying to express those kinds of emotions, the major 3rd is an interval that you might want to avoid. However, if you stack two major 3rds (forming an augmented triad, see p. 14), you can actually make a creepy-sounding chord that is quite usable in extreme metal. Making the right combinations of notes is very important.

As a bassist in extreme metal, you may occasionally want to play two or more notes simultaneously. Two notes played together are called *double stops*—anything more than two generally is called a *chord*. Playing chords and double stops in unison with your guitarist can really add power to the riff you're playing. Alternatively, you can play the notes individually and create a cool bass line using the notes of the chords the guitarist is playing. It's up to you to decide which approach works better for any given part.

Here are some intervals and chords you'll find useful for creating extreme metal riffs and bass lines.

Perfect 5th

Played together, this interval creates the *power chord*, the most common guitar chord in metal. The "5" chord (p. 14) is really the same chord, with an added octave.

Diminished 5th (Tritone)

The augmented 4th/diminished 5th is also called the *tritone* because it consists of three whole steps. The tritone probably is the darkest-sounding and, therefore, most important interval in extreme metal. You'll notice that it appears often in the scales in this chapter and in the music throughout this book. This interval is more often encountered as part of a riff, rather than played simultaneously as a chord, although the chord can be found in metal as well—mainly in progressive or avant-garde metal.

Augmented 5th

The augmented 5th is another dissonant, dark-sounding interval. It is a key part of the sound of the whole-tone scale. It also illustrates why the order of notes can be so important, because you'll see that, if you invert (reverse the order) of the notes in the interval, you'll wind up with the much happier-sounding major 3rd.

Minor 3rd

Comprised of the root and the 3rd of a minor scale, the minor 3rd is another very common interval in extreme metal due to its dark, sad quality. You'll notice it is part of every scale shown in this book with the exception of the whole-tone scale.

Octave

The octave is so named because it is the interval between the first and eighth degrees of a seven-note diatonic scale. It's the same note as the root, just higher. So, for example, the E at the end of the E natural minor scale is an octave higher than the E root note. When played separately, octaves may sound dangerously close to disco and should be used with caution, but played together, especially as part of a darkly melodic riff, they can be truly creepy-sounding.

Example 1-9:

And here are some chords that you'll find useful in extreme metal.

"5" Chord (Power Chord)

As mentioned previously, this chord is created by stacking a perfect 5th above a root. The root is commonly doubled an octave higher as well.

Diminished 5th (with Octave Added)

You can think of this as a power chord with a flatted 5th. It's very evil-sounding and creates a lot of tension.

Augmented Triad

This triad is two major 3rds stacked to create one cool, dissonant chord. This chord is found all over the whole-tone scale, as well as in the harmonic minor scale, where it is comprised of the scale's 3rd, 5th, and 7th degrees. This is good to know if you want to add a little dissonance to a neo-classical harmonic minor riff.

Minor Triad

This triad is a minor 3rd and a perfect 5th played together. It's a very somber-sounding chord and is most commonly found in black metal and melodic death metal, but it can be found in virtually every sub-genre of metal.

Example 1-10:

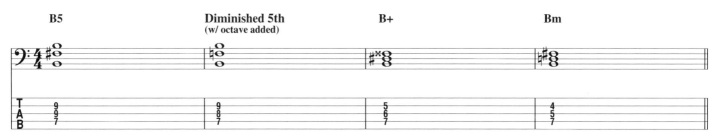

CHAPTER 2:

RIGHT-HAND TECHNIQUES

In this chapter, we will cover two common approaches to plucking the bass with your fingers: the two-finger and three-finger approaches. If you develop a good grasp of these techniques, you should be able to handle all of the play-along examples presented in chapters 5 through 10. Just about everything I play features some combination of these techniques.

TWO-FINGER PLUCKING

Two-finger plucking on the bass is the most common of all of the plucking techniques. It's usually the first way bassists are taught to play, as it is the most natural and intuitive; alternating your index and middle fingers should come fairly naturally for most people. Two-finger plucking really is the "meat and potatoes" of bass playing.

This example will help you develop your alternate two-finger plucking technique. Try to strictly alternate between your index and middle fingers, even when crossing strings. You'll notice that every four bars of this exercise contain the first three notes of a diminished arpeggio, starting on the open B string. This is the first of many exercises you'll find in this book that features a diminished tonality.

Example 2-1:

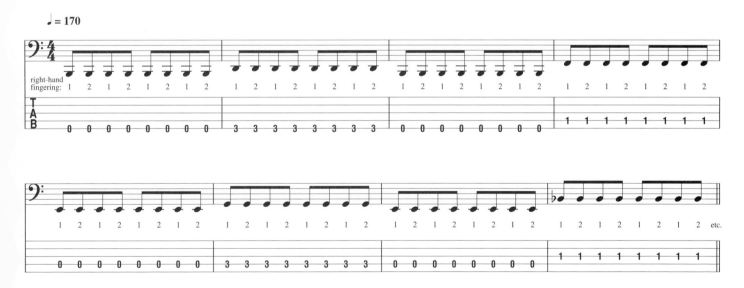

Here's an example written with the B half/whole diminished scale. Try to stick with strict alternation between your fingers for this one as well. You may find that you have a tendency to rake (play with the same finger) the notes when returning to the E string after playing a note on the A string. This technique is completely acceptable, but for now, try to avoid it so as to fully develop your alternate plucking.

Example 2-2:

This example will help you to develop your string-crossing technique. Try the three different plucking patterns shown between the notation and tab staves to see which works best for you. In time, your fingers will choose the most comfortable pattern without you even realizing it, but for now, practice each variation slowly before moving on and completing the whole example. This example was written with the B harmonic minor scale.

Example 2-3:

THREE-FINGER PLUCKING: GALLOPING AND TRIPLET PATTERNS

If you're new to three-finger plucking, I recommend that you start with galloping and triplet patterns. The reason for this is simple: three-note patterns lend themselves to three-finger plucking. With practice, the following examples should feel quite natural.

This example shows the first variation of the classic "gallop." This version includes an eighth note, followed by two sixteenth notes. For this variation, lead with your index finger, followed quickly by your ring and middle fingers.

Example 2-4:

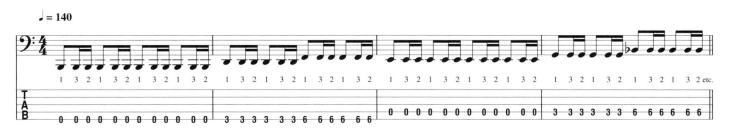

The second of the two classic gallops, this example features the grouping of two sixteenth notes, followed by an eighth note. This time, you will lead with your ring finger, followed by the middle and index.

Example 2-5:

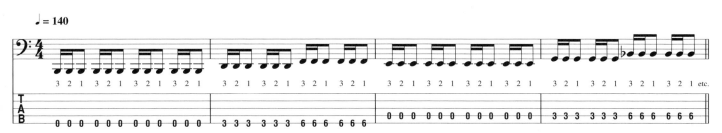

Now we introduce the triplet, which, unlike the gallop, features three notes of equal duration. I often hear people erroneously calling the gallop patterns "triplets" because the gallop features three notes as well. I've also heard the term "Bonanza triplets" used to describe the gallop (named after the popular TV show's galloping theme song). It's not the correct term, but I have to say, I get a laugh out of it. At any rate, a genuine triplet is three evenly-spaced notes occupying the space of two. In this example, there are three triplet eighth notes for every beat in place of two regular eighth notes.

Practice this example slowly. It will take time for you to really play these evenly, and you may be tempted to play these triplet patterns with two alternating fingers, rather than three. Avoid this, as the purpose of this exercise is to develop your three-finger plucking technique—not to play slow triplets with two fingers.

Example 2-6:

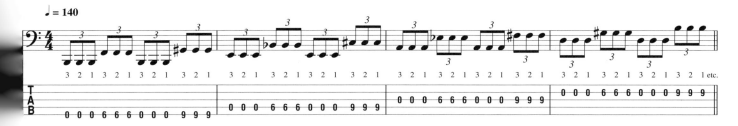

Now we'll start working on playing triplets while crossing the strings. This example uses augmented 5ths.

Example 2-7:

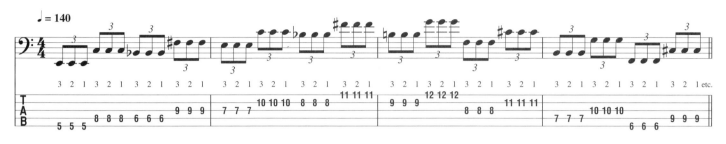

Here is a triplet example that features *string skipping*. String skipping is a bit more difficult than simply crossing the strings in sequence, as you have to avoid bumping into the string you're skipping. If you bump the skipped string, it will create a lot of extra string noise, which, of course, is not what you want.

Example 2-8:

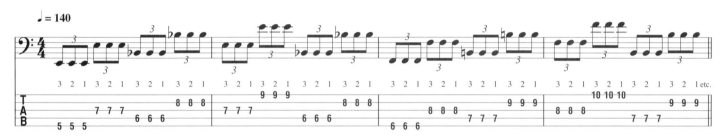

Now let's switch back to the gallop. This time, we'll divide each three-note group between two strings to further develop your string-crossing technique.

Example 2-9:

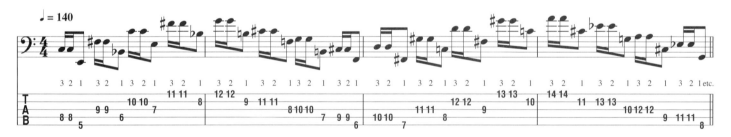

Here is a galloping pattern similar to the last example, but featuring a string skip. Again, you'll have to do some work to control the extra noise. As always, practice this slowly with a metronome and gradually build up the speed. Never practice something faster than you can cleanly play it!

Example 2-10:

THREE-FINGER PLUCKING: SIXTEENTH NOTES

If there is one technique that people ask me about the most, it's this one. Being able to play fast and even sixteenth-note patterns with three-finger plucking is very useful in extreme metal. Fast alternate-picked guitar parts are very common in this kind of music; if you want to keep up with them without using a pick, these techniques can be a lifesaver.

To begin, let's work on getting the right hand solid before we even add pitches to the left hand. Lightly cover the strings with your left hand to mute the strings, concentrating specifically on what's happening with your right hand. You'll notice that the fingering repeatedly goes: ring, middle, index. As you saw earlier in the chapter, this plucking pattern easily lends itself to groups of three, like triplets and gallops. Now, for these sixteenth-note groups, you'll need to create a feeling of "four" for each beat. The best way to do this is to slightly accent every fourth note. So, this pattern will cycle every twelve notes, as shown below (accented notes in CAPS):

RING, middle, index, ring, MIDDLE, index, ring, middle, INDEX, ring, middle, index, etc.

Example 2-11:

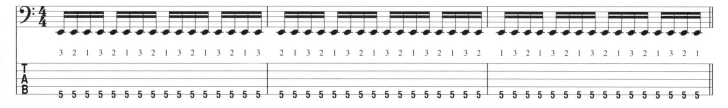

Now that you're starting to get a feel for the sixteenth-note pulse, let's try adding a fretted pitch: E on the B string.

Example 2-12:

Here we start to move things around a little bit on the B string. I've found this particular exercise to be very useful for developing a feeling of four.

Example 2-13:

In this example, we'll begin to work on string crossing. This exercise uses the A harmonic minor scale.

Example 2-14:

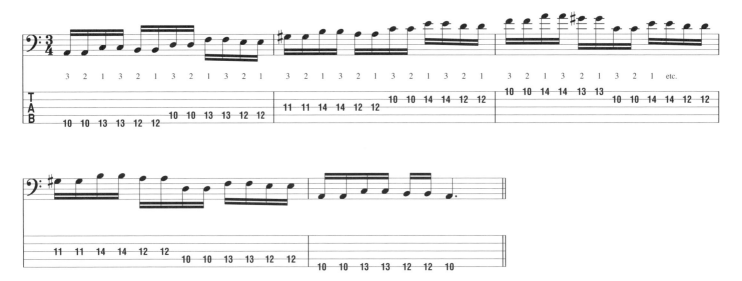

This example is fairly tricky. It, too, features the A harmonic minor scale, but this time, you'll be playing two notes per pitch instead of four. So, you'll get to the end of the exercise twice as fast!

Example 2-15:

Now let's try the A harmonic minor scale, playing each note only once. Once you get to the point where you can play individual notes with the three-finger plucking technique, you'll really have it mastered.

Example 2-16:

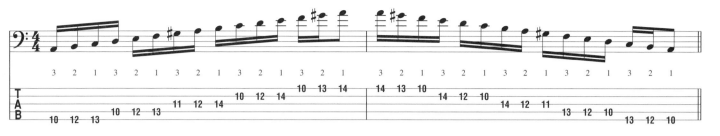

Next I'm going to introduce a second technique for playing sixteenth notes with three-finger plucking. This technique features a much shorter pattern for the right hand. You start the pattern the same way as the twelve-note-cycle approach (ring, middle, index), but then, instead of going to your ring finger, you go back to the middle, as shown:

RING, middle, index, middle, RING, middle, index, middle, etc.

This technique is great for a group of four sixteenth notes that is split in half between two strings, as this example illustrates.

Example 2-17:

Four-note-per-string patterns are another situation where the "return to middle" technique of playing sixteenth notes can be applied with great success.

Example 2-18:

CHAPTER 3:
LEFT-HAND TECHNIQUES

In this chapter, we'll briefly cover some techniques to help build finger independence and strength in your fret hand.

The following examples show various patterns that will help you to develop your finger independence. Use one finger per fret for these exercises. For example, look at the first few bars of Example 3-1. You'll want to assign the first fret to your fret hand's index finger, the second to your middle, the third to your ring, and the fourth to your pinky. Using that same pattern, take all of these examples up and down the neck. I like to play them to the twelfth fret and back down, but you can go even higher on the neck if you like.

Example 3-1:

Example 3-2:

Example 3-3:

Example 3-4:

This next example is a combination of the first four examples. It's quite a handful, but will leave you well-prepared for any strange patterns your guitarist might throw at you. After you get these examples down, try creating new ones with your own patterns. These examples might not be the most musical-sounding patterns in the world, but then again, a cool dissonant pattern can often work very well in extreme metal. While devising your own practice patterns, you may very well stumble onto a great riff idea.

Example 3-5:

etc.

Another option for finger independence exercises is to throw string skipping into the mix, as I have done here with this simple octave pattern. Once again, you can create several of your own patterns like this and combine them to make all sorts of chops-busting exercises. If you get used to these kinds of exercises, normal scale patterns will seem easy.

Example 3-6:

This next example is a legato exercise designed to increase your fret-hand strength. Pluck the first note of each measure and then let your fret hand do the rest of the work. Be careful not to over-exert yourself while practicing this, as it can really tire your hand out in short order. Don't risk injury; take your time and gradually build up your strength.

Example 3-7:

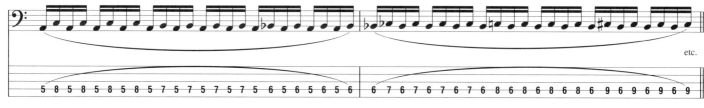

CHAPTER 4:

TAPPING

So far, this book has covered some fairly traditional bass playing techniques for both the right and left hands. Sure, three-finger plucking might be somewhat uncommon, but it's really not a flashy technique. So, keeping in mind that you might want to learn some of the flashier techniques that I've used over the years, I decided to include a chapter on tapping.

I'd like to start by saying that the basic mechanics of all of these moves are techniques that I learned years ago from recordings and instructional materials released by other bassists, like Billy Sheehan, Stu Hamm, Beaver Felton, and Wally Voss. Although I've taken these techniques and used them in my own way, I'm obviously not the one who invented them. Chances are, once you learn these techniques, you too will find interesting new ways to apply them to your own music. Learn the techniques and then make them your own.

While practicing these exercises, as with the other chapters, start out slowly and work your way up. You'll be absolutely amazed by how fast and fluid these licks can sound once you have them under your fingers.

HAMMER/PULL TAPPING

The first type of tapping that I was exposed to was what I like to call "hammer/pull tapping." I call it that because the sound is produced by tapping a note (or notes) with your right hand and pulling off other notes with your left. This is a very common type of tapping that also is frequently seen on guitar. Check out Billy Sheehan's work to see true mastery of this style of tapping.

This example is an extremely common tapping pattern. In this case, we are outlining a diminished 7th arpeggio but, of course, you could substitute any number of different arpeggios or note groupings while still using the same basic motion.

Example 4-1:

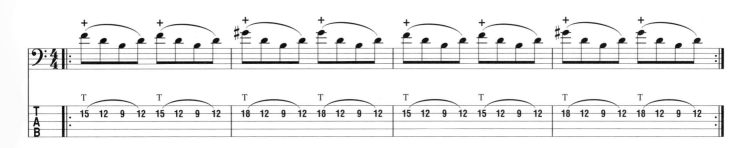

This pattern is a slight variation of the previous example. The variation creates a triplet feel.

Example 4-2:

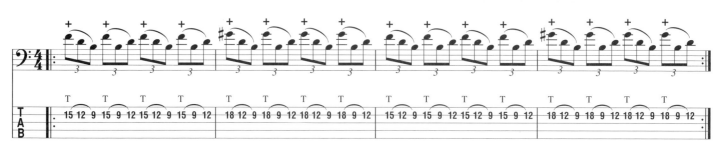

Here's a sixteenth-note pattern that uses the whole-tone scale. This example will really work your left hand, so once again, my warning not to overdo it is appropriate.

Example 4-3:

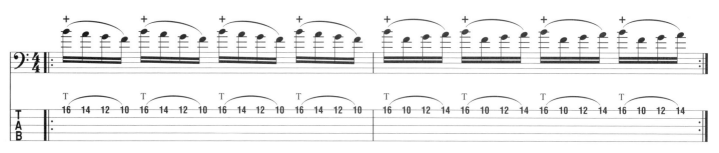

Here's another variation of Example 4-3. In this case, you alternate the ascending and descending pattern every beat instead of every measure.

Example 4-4:

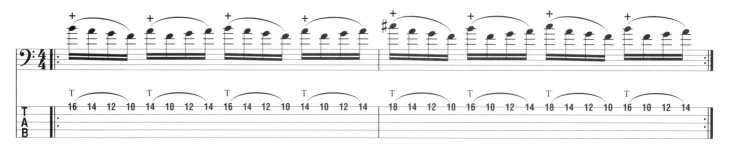

Here's a cool lick that uses the D whole/half diminished scale. Example 4-5 works you through the first two moves in the lick, while Example 4-6 expands upon that pattern, going up and down the scale. This pattern sounds fantastic once you have it up to speed.

Example 4-5:

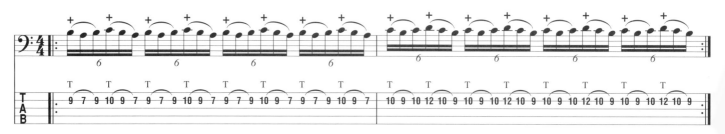

Example 4-6:

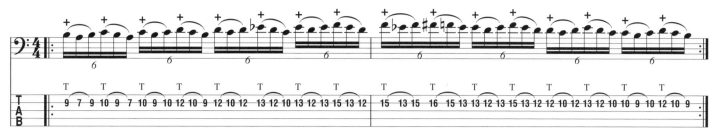

PRESS TAPPING

The second main type of tapping is something I like to call "press tapping." I call it that because the sound is generated by simply pressing (tapping) your fingertip on the fretboard at the location of the note you want to hear. Some people call these "hammer-ons from nowhere." With this type of tapping, there are no notes pulled off or hammered on in the traditional sense. Stu Hamm is one of the first—and best—practitioners of this style of tapping.

Here's a basic press-tapping exercise that uses perfect 4ths and 5ths. It's not a very heavy- or dark-sounding lick, but it's simple and will help you to learn the basics of this technique.

Example 4-7:

The next example uses octaves and diminished 5ths. I really enjoy the sound that is created by tapping these intervals and have used it a few times over the years. This type of pattern can be used to create blazing fast sixteenth-note runs. It works well in both soloing and supporting situations.

Example 4-8:

Here's a power chord press-tapping pattern—first with the 5th and octave ascending, then descending.

Example 4-9:

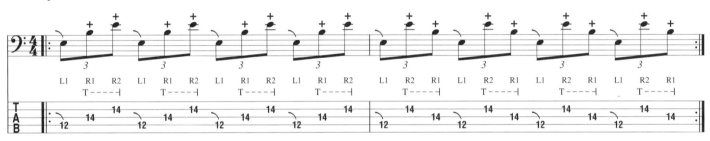

Here's a basic four-note arpeggio tapping pattern. This is another very versatile technique that can be applied to numerous arpeggios and note groupings. Experiment and have fun.

Example 4-10:

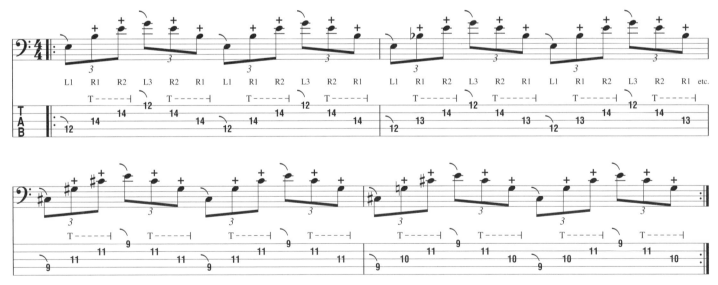

THREE-STRING SWEEPS

This technique is not a pure tapping technique but rather a hybrid of three-finger pluck-ing, raking, and tapping. The effect of this technique sounds very similar to a sweep-picked arpeggio, so I've decided to call it a three-string sweep, although strictly speaking, it's actu-ally not a sweep. As far as I know, Billy Sheehan invented this technique. It has become one of my favorites over the years, and I think you'll enjoy it, too. Out of all of the techniques illustrated in this chapter, this one might have the biggest "wow" factor. Once you get it up to speed, you'll definitely be turning some heads.

This example illustrates the technique step-by-step, starting with the plucked portion. Although you'll be plucking the notes on the fretboard, you will *not* be tapping them. There is only one tapped note in this technique. After the plucked portion, you hammer on a note and then tap the highest note. In the next example, you will learn how to return to the starting point to complete the "sweep."

Example 4-11:

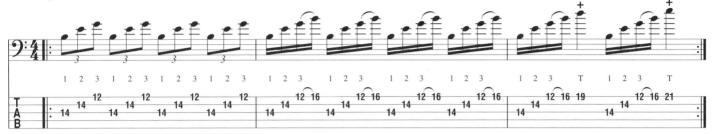

This example illustrates the whole sweep. When you get to the tapped note, tap and release via the "hammer/pull" method shown earlier in the chapter, then rake the last note with your index finger (this will be the same finger that you tapped with) to return to the starting point. This example uses a minor arpeggio.

Example 4-12:

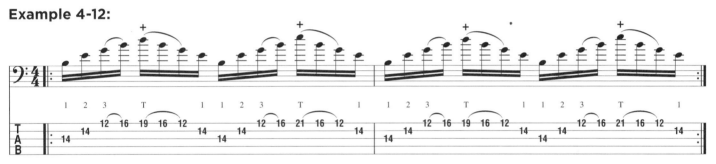

These next two examples use the exact same mechanics as Example 4-12; however, instead of the minor scale, these figures utilize the whole-tone scale (4-13) and diminished 7th arpeggio (4-14).

Example 4-13:

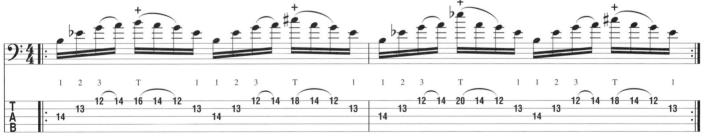

Example 4-14:

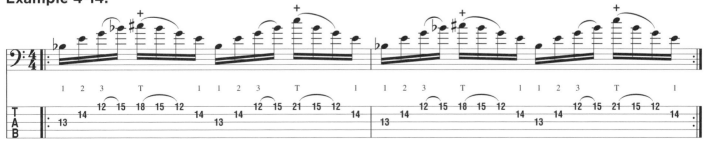

Part 2: APPLICATION

CHAPTER 5:

RHYTHM EXERCISES

A good sense of rhythm in your plucking hand is an extremely important yet often over-looked facet of metal bass playing. I've found that most players spend a lot of time practicing scale patterns, but rarely practice material that would help develop their sense of rhythm. In my opinion, you should be focusing equally on both melodic practicing (e.g., scales and arpeggios) and rhythmic practicing (exercises like the ones in this chapter).

When you start to learn each example, begin by playing it twice—first using the two-finger plucking technique and then with the three-finger plucking technique. Listen to how the part sounds with each approach and try to come up with a combination of the two that sounds good and feels comfortable. Also, keep in mind that there may be a few parts that are too fast for you to play with only two fingers. In those cases, the three-finger technique is the obvious choice.

As you work through the examples, creating these plucking combinations will gradually become second nature for you. The goal here is to create such a strong natural sense of rhythm in your right hand that you don't even have to think about which finger is doing what. You should eventually be able to just feel the rhythm.

Tip: You can practice these rhythms just about anywhere by tapping your fingers on a hard surface, like a table top. Although the attack that you'll be using will be a lot different (most likely much lighter) than if you were plucking the part on your bass, this technique will help you to internalize the rhythm that you're working on. It's a great way to practice when you don't have a bass handy; just make sure that you're not driving the people around you nuts with all of that tapping!

Let's get started with a common triplet rhythm. This type of rhythm usually is heard in tradi-tional heavy metal.

Example 5-1:

FB = Full Band
GDO = Guitar/Drums Only

Tr. 2   FB
Tr. 3   GDO

Here's the same rhythm again but with notes from the E diminished 7th arpeggio replacing the open E on every other beat. Throughout this chapter, you can add notes to the exercises in this way to make them more interesting—but don't do this until you've already mastered the basic open E string version.

Example 5-2:

Here's a basic pattern that uses eighth notes and gallop note groupings. This type of pattern commonly is heard in thrash metal.

Example 5-3:

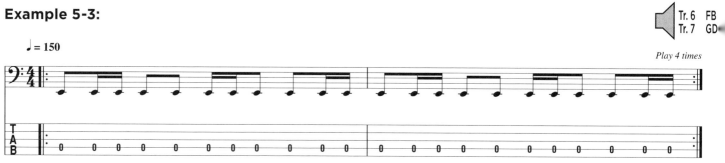

Like Example 5-3, these next two patterns can be found in thrash metal. The addition of note groupings featuring four sixteenth notes adds rhythmic interest to the part. I have found that, for parts like these, using two-finger technique for the beats with eighth notes and three-finger technique for the beats with gallop or straight sixteenth-note groups works best, especially at higher tempos.

Example 5-4:

Example 5-5:

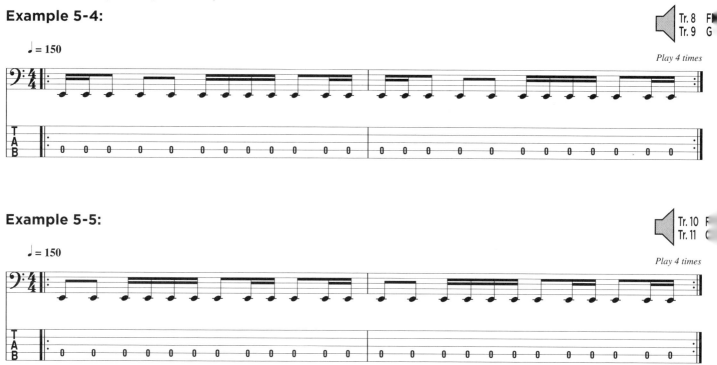

This example combines gallop and sixteenth-note groups in a way that creates groups of six consecutive sixteenth notes.

Example 5-6:

Tr. 12 FB
Tr. 13 GDO

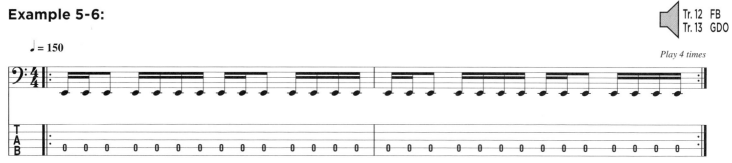

In these next examples, a new note grouping is introduced: the sixteenth note/eighth note/sixteenth note () grouping. It has a more syncopated feel to it than the gallop, although it comprises the same three note values. Patterns featuring this grouping became common in the nineties with the rise of nü metal and metalcore.

Example 5-7:

Tr. 14 FB
Tr. 15 GDO

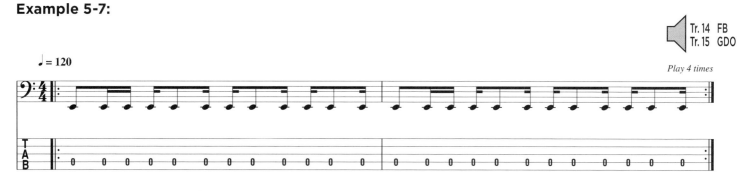

Example 5-8:

Tr. 16 FB
Tr. 17 GDO

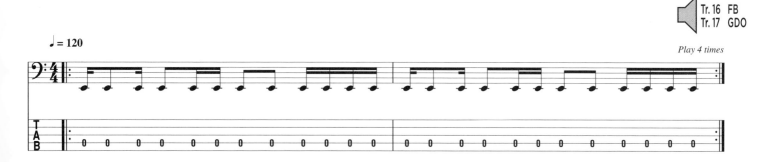

Example 5-9:

Tr. 18 FB
Tr. 19 GDO

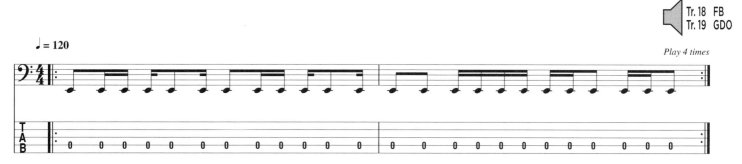

At first glance, this next example might look extremely long and complicated, but on closer inspection, it will become clear that it's actually a simple repetition of this note grouping: one eighth note and three sixteenth notes (♪♬).

The bass plays this pattern repeatedly over the drummer's 4/4 beat until it cycles back to the beginning, which takes five measures.

Example 5-10:

Tr. 20 FB
Tr. 21 GDO

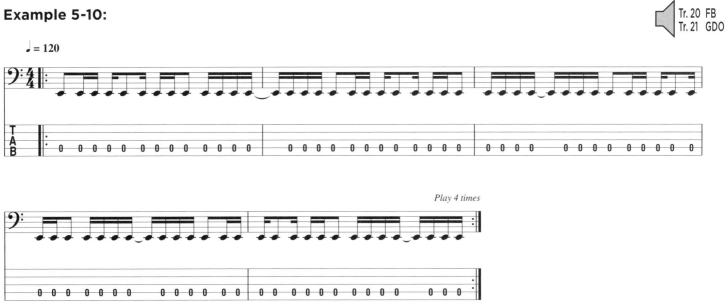

Play 4 times

Like the previous example, this pattern features a short group of notes being played repeatedly over a 4/4 drum pattern. The note grouping is two eighth notes and three sixteenth notes (♪♪♬).

This time, it will take two more bars of 4/4 to get back to a point where this note grouping begins on beat 1 of a given measure.

Example 5-11:

Tr. 22 FB
Tr. 23 GDC

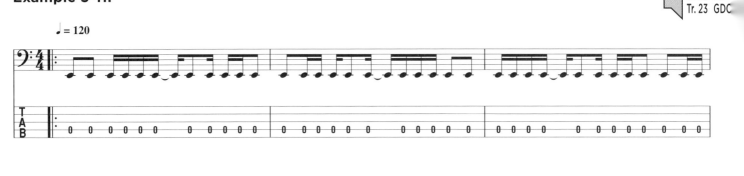

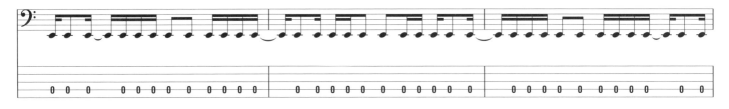

Play 4 times

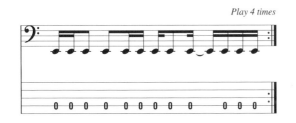

Patterns like the ones shown in Examples 5-10 and 5-11 feature *polymeter*, meaning that there are two meters being used at the same time. In Example 5-10, the bass guitar and the kick drums are playing sixteen measures of 5/16, while the drummer's hands (snare and cymbals) are playing five measures of 4/4. In Example 5-11, the relationship is sixteen measures of 7/16 against seven measures of 4/4.

It can take time to become comfortable with parts like these. I recommend that you start by focusing on the kick drums as a guide. Once you feel completely locked in to that basic pattern, you can start to pay more attention to the drummer's hands. But be careful—it can be easy to get lost while playing polyrhythms and polymeters.

To hear more examples of this type, check out Meshuggah. They were one of the first bands in extreme metal to use polymeter extensively.

CHAPTER 6:

TRIPLET GROOVES

Riffs with a triplet feel are very common in the various forms of extreme metal. In this chapter, we'll take a look at three riffs based on triplets.

This example is a simple eighth-note triplet groove based on a diminished scale. Notice how the bass line locks in with the ride cymbal throughout the part.

Example 6-1:

Tr. 24 FB
Tr. 25 GDC

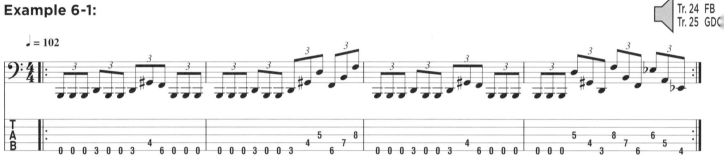

In this exercise, a new rhythmic unit is introduced: a triplet containing an eighth note, two sixteenth notes, and another eighth note (♪♫♪).

This rhythmic unit creates a gallop feel within the triplet. The bass line closely follows the kick-drum pattern until the fourth measure. At that point, the kick drums play a straight pattern, while the bass continues the same triplet/gallop feel. The guitar and bass parts are written with the E whole-tone scale.

Example 6-2:

Tr. 26 FB
Tr. 27 G

This next example features a drum beat that is informally called the "bomb blast," which consists of a blast beat that leads with the snare and features fast double bass rather than the kick/snare alternation found in a traditional blast beat. The actual pulse of the part is not really that fast (♩ = 136), but it sounds quite frantic since there are three snare and six kick strikes per beat. The bass line stays with the snare drum throughout much of the pattern, with the only rhythmic variation being the triplet/gallop in the third, fourth, and seventh measures.

In the first two examples of this chapter, the bass and guitar parts basically are the same, but the increased tempo of this example compelled me to write an independent bass line. I will break down what went into the composition of this bass line, measure-by-measure:

- In the first two measures, the guitar plays sixteenth-note sextuplets. If your plucking technique is exceptionally fast or you play with a pick, you could try to match this note-for-note, but I felt a better option was to play half as many notes; in other words, the bass will play eighth-note triplets. This reinforces the snare drum while also playing the same melody as the guitar.

- In measures 3 and 4, the guitar accents some notes on the low-E string while pedaling on the B string. Again, rather than try to match the guitar part's picking note-for-note, I've created a bass line that reinforces the rhythm of the part while also following the melody of the guitar.

- Measures 5 and 6 feature the same guitar part as measures 1 and 2, but to create interest, I decided to add some more notes to the part. The rhythm stays the same (eighth-note triplets), but now the bass begins to utilize other notes of the scale in which the part was written (B harmonic minor). When writing bass lines like these, it really helps to know the scale in which the guitar part was written. If you can't identify the scale yourself, ask your guitar player. Once you know the scale that is being used, you can add harmonic interest to your bass line by playing various intervals rather than simple unisons.

- Measure 7 was created via the same process that was used for measures 3 and 4 and, therefore, has the same rhythm. Measure 8 returns to the simple eighth-note triplet rhythm and outlines the guitar part, with a few minor 3rds thrown in to add interest.

Example 6-3:

Tr. 28 FB
Tr. 29 GDO

CHAPTER 7:
SIXTEENTH-NOTE GROOVES

A sixteenth-note groove accompanied by a double-bass kick-drum pattern is one of the most common musical ideas in extreme metal. Whereas the triplet patterns covered in the last chapter create a feel of three notes per beat, sixteenth-note patterns create a feeling of four.

Here's a pattern written with the B whole/half diminished scale. The bass line stays with the kick the entire time, using legato hammer/pull technique during the sextuplet sections. The legato passages should be easy for you if you've been practicing Example 3-7.

Example 7-1:

Tr. 30
Tr. 31

In the first four bars of Example 7-2, the bass line follows the kick and snare. Since the tempo is fairly slow and the kick and snare pattern is fairly sparse, I decided to sustain some of the notes rather than keep their duration the same as the kick or snare with which they're associated. The notes played during these measures match what the guitar is doing at the time of the kick or snare strikes. The scale used is the B whole-tone scale.

When the double-kick pattern begins, the bass line plays in unison with guitar, creating a more powerful, driving feel. Building up the bass line and drum part in this way can create a much more dynamic effect than merely playing the same beat and unison bass line throughout.

Example 7-2:

This next bass line was created with similar logic to that of the previous example: a relatively sparse traditional bass line followed by a driving unison line. Since the tempo is fairly quick, the bass line for the first four measures sounds fine with notes that are the same duration as the kick drum. Also, because there are so many notes in the kick pattern, adding more notes to the bass line on the snare strikes seemed unnecessary. The scale used for this pattern is B half/whole diminished.

Example 7-3:

Tr. 34 FB
Tr. 35 GDO

This example features the same bass line building technique that is utilized in Examples 7-2 and 7-3. The main difference here is that, when the bass line switches from syncopated to unison, the drum beat plays a double-time thrash beat rather than a double-kick pattern. The scale used in this pattern is E Hungarian minor.

Example 7-4:

Tr. 36 F♯
Tr. 37 G♭

CHAPTER 8

WRITING BASS LINES FOR SPEED-PICKED GUITAR PARTS

If you're an extreme metal bassist who has made the decision to play fingerstyle, you've undoubtedly had to face the challenge of what to do during a speed-picked guitar part. When guitarists use alternate picking to tremolo pick or play fast sixteenth-note patterns, they can end up leaving even the fastest fingerstyle player in the dust. Even if the bassist is able to keep up with the guitarist, the result is often an uneven and largely inaudible jumble of notes. In this chapter, we're going to look at two different speed-picked dual guitar parts and examine various options for creating bass lines that complement them.

Example 8-1 illustrates the safest approach, by far: playing "half time." By playing eighth notes instead of sixteenths, like the guitar, you will be playing one note for every two notes the guitarist plays. This may not be the most exciting approach to take, but it might be the best choice—particularly at high tempos, whereby playing sixteenths in unison with the guitarist is beyond your ability. This approach usually yields a tight and completely acceptable bass line—but not always a very interesting one.

Since there are two guitar parts in Example 8-1, you'll have two notes from which to choose when creating your bass line. In this case, I've chosen to create a line in which the bass plays either the root of a minor 3rd interval or the high note of an octave. As far as the minor 3rds go, had I decided to play the 3rd rather than the root, it would actually create more of a major 6th feel. While emphasizing the major 6th could be an interesting option, generally in metal, the minor tonality works best. Remember, as the bassist, you will be determining the root of all chords and harmonies. Choose your notes carefully!

Example 8-1:

Track 42 contains the guitar and drums only for Examples 8-1 through 8-4

Tr. 38 FB

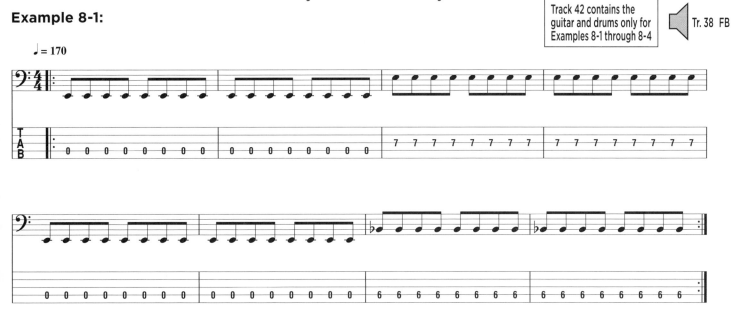

With respect to note choice, Example 8-2 is identical to Example 8-1. The only difference between the parts is here the bass is playing sixteenth notes along with the guitars and drums. Take special care to avoid "flamming" with the kick drums. I use the term "flam" loosely here, but basically it means you're not playing exactly in time with the kick drums and, thus, creating accidental grace notes. Flamming will make you and your drummer sound sloppy—not good! So, practice this exercise slowly at first and then build up to speed to really get locked in with the kick drums.

Example 8-2:

Track 42 contains the guitar and drums only for Examples 8-1 through 8-4

Tr. 39 FB

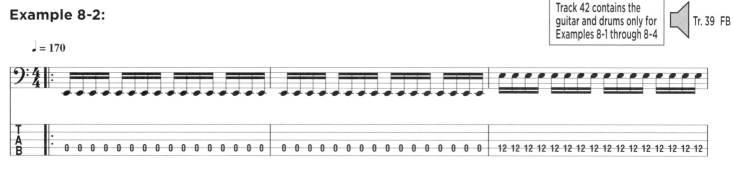

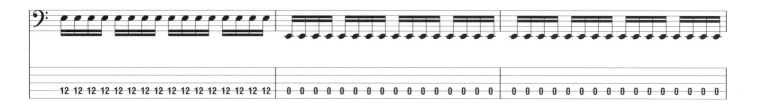

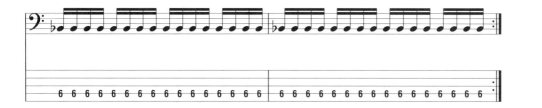

This chapter's third example slows the pulse back down to eighth notes, but adds some more variety via its note choices. Basically, this line was composed with notes from the parts for both guitars 1 and 2. This is a great approach to take when the sixteenth notes being played by the guitar and/or kick drums have surpassed your top finger-picking speeds. It's a relatively slow line, but it's still interesting to listen to.

Example 8-3:

Track 42 contains the guitar and drums only for Examples 8-1 through 8-4

Tr. 40

This next example illustrates how a technique typically associated with soloing can be used in a supporting role. Because press tapping can generate an extremely fast and precise flurry of sixteenth notes, it can work well with guitar riffs like the one in this example. Once again, the notes played by the bass are derived entirely from the guitar part.

Example 8-4:

Track 42 contains the guitar and drums only for Examples 8-1 through 8-4

Tr. 41 FB
Tr. 42 GDO

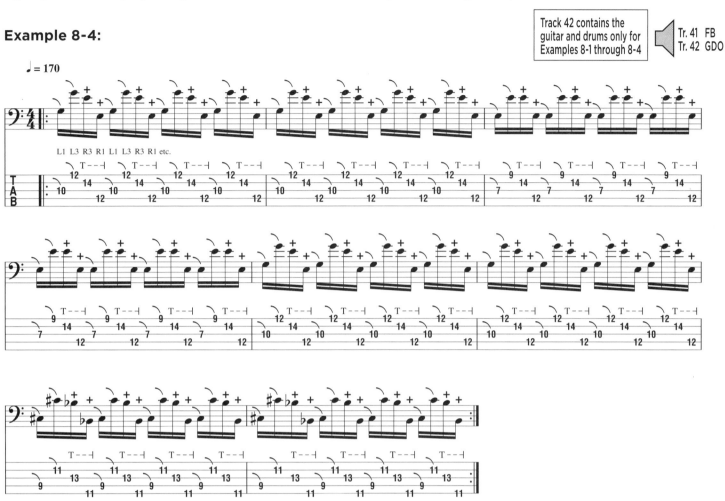

Example 8-5 is the first example of the second guitar pattern featured in this chapter. The scale used for this pattern is B harmonic minor. The bass line was created in the same manner as that in Example 8-1: the bass plays an eighth-note pattern that uses the root note of each implied 3rd, some of which are major this time around.

Example 8-5:

Track 47 contains the guitar and drums only for Examples 8-5 through 8-8

Tr. 43 FB

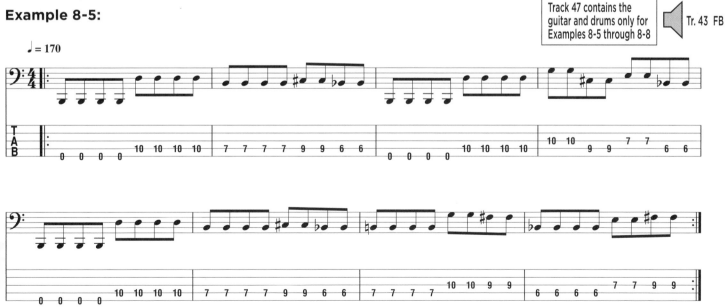

The bass line in Example 8-6 was created in the same manner as the one in Example 8-2. It uses the same notes as Example 8-5 (some voiced an octave higher for clarity), but this time the bass plays a tremolo-picked pattern in unison with the guitar.

Tremolo picking is a term that refers to the rapid articulation of a single note. Tremolo picking is used extensively in extreme metal—particularly in the sub-genre death metal, where it is used to create a feeling of speed during a slow melody, like this one. At high tempos, each string player in the band might be tremolo picking at a slightly different rate (basically, everyone is playing as fast as they can), but at a moderate tempo, like the one used in this example, the tremolo picking essentially is sixteenth notes.

Do your best to keep your picking steady and even, especially during the brief double-bass bursts. If the parts sound too jumbled, you might want to try one of the other approaches covered in this chapter.

Example 8-6:

Track 47 contains the guitar and drums only for Examples 8-5 through 8-8 | Tr. 44 F

Like Example 8-3, this bass line was created by using a combination of notes from the two guitar parts. If there were only one guitar part, you could still create a line like this if you know the scale the guitarist used to create the part (see Example 6-3).

Example 8-7:

Track 47 contains the guitar and drums only for Examples 8-5 through 8-8 | Tr. 45

This next example illustrates how you can compose an interesting bass line by using a combination of the lines from Examples 8-6 and 8-7. The majority of the line is the same as the melodic eighth-note pattern in Example 8-7, but it switches to the three-finger speed picking of Example 8-6 during the short bursts of sixteenth notes played on the kick drums.

Example 8-8:

Track 47 contains the guitar and drums only for Examples 8-5 through 8-8

Tr. 46 FB
Tr. 47 GDO

CHAPTER 9:

DOOM AND SLUDGE

In this chapter, we'll take a look at the slower side of extreme metal. Slow riffs played on low-tuned instruments can be incredibly heavy-sounding. Riffs like these can be used by bands from any of the various genres of extreme metal, and there are also several sub-genres that are entirely dedicated to playing slow, back-breakingly heavy music. The words "doom" and "sludge" are often used when describing these genres (e.g., "death doom" to describe a death metal band that predominantly uses slow tempos). But let's not get too caught up in genre names; instead, let's get down to the business of making great bass lines for these plodding, ultra-heavy riffs.

Example 9-1 is a simple riff based on the B diminished scale. One of the great things about these slower doom-type riffs is that they leave a lot of space for bass fills, like the ones shown in the second, fourth, and sixth measures of this example. Although the riff is written with the diminished scale, I thought the blues scale scale sounded good during the sustained chords that the guitars are playing in these measures. However, instead of using the B blues scale, I chose to use the scale that matched the chord being sustained (C# blues in measures 2 and 6; F blues in measure 4).

These little fills definitely are inspired by players like Geezer Butler (basically, the master and creator of this style) and also by Steve DiGiorgio's work on the first album by doom-influenced death metal legends Autopsy. Once you have learned the fills as written, feel free to go back and improvise your own over the guitar pattern. Creating fills with the pentatonic or blues scale is easy and can be a lot of fun.

Example 9-1:

Tr. 48 F
Tr. 49 G

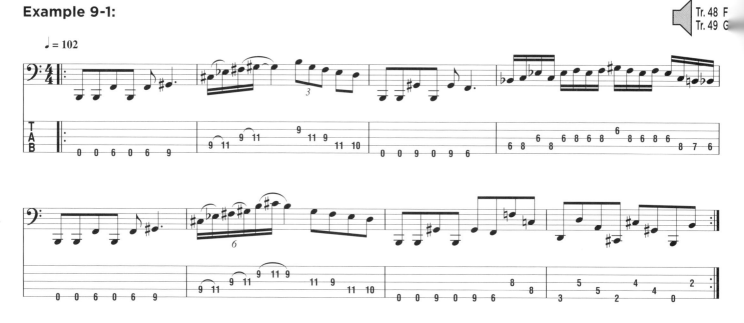

This next example is a bit more complicated than the previous one. It uses the B Hungarian minor scale, and there is less space in which to improvise fills in this example, so I chose to follow the guitar part closely, even playing octave chords where appropriate. For the trills in the fourth measure, you might have a hard time playing perfectly straight sextuplets. But don't worry much about that; the trill effect will still sound good, even if you're not completely locked in. Just get it as close as you can.

Example 9-2:

Tr. 50 FB
Tr. 51 GDO

The guitar part for this next example is the same as the part in Example 9-2; however, the drum pattern has switched to an eighth-note double-bass pattern. This time, the bass line follows the kick drums very closely and adds notes from the B Hungarian minor scale throughout the line to add variety and flavor.

Example 9-3:

Tr. 52 FB
Tr. 53 GDO

CHAPTER 10

SONG EXAMPLES

ow that you've learned some of the most common techniques used in extreme metal and worked through a number of riff ideas typical of the genre, you should be ready to play some complete songs. I've written three short songs for this chapter, each of them incorporating some of the techniques and compositional tools that you've learned in the previous chapters.

In addition to reinforcing what you've already learned, playing through these examples will help to build your endurance. Even a simple riff can become difficult if it's played at a high tempo and/or for an extended period of time, so developing your endurance is very important. I've found that the best way to do this is by playing complete songs. I think that having the clearly-defined goal of reaching the end of a song will discipline you as a musician in a way open-ended scale practicing cannot. Beyond that, playing songs is usually a lot more fun than merely practicing dry scale and arpeggio exercises. Both are important and should be part of your practice routine, but chances are, you'll spend a lot more time on something that you're enjoying than on something that's boring you. The key is to compose challenging exercises that also are fun. That is what I've attempted to do with the song examples in this chapter (and also throughout the entire book). Hopefully, you'll be having so much fun while playing the songs that you won't realize how hard you're practicing!

SONG EXAMPLE 1

This song is a fairly simple thrash song. It seemed appropriate to start off with this example since thrash is often considered the first true extreme metal genre.

Song Structure and Performance Notes

Section A (Intro):   The song starts off with the guitar playing the verse riff while the bass and drums accent the power chords in the riff.

Section B (Verse):   Here, the bass and guitar basically play in unison, with the only difference being that the bass only plays the roots of the power chords, rather than the whole chord. If you have trouble playing the sixteenth-note open E pedal tone, see Chapter 8 for some possible alternatives, or play the part with a plectrum. The verse riff was written with the E minor scale.

Section C (Chorus):   Here, the meter switches to 3/4, and the bass and guitar play a galloping diminished arpeggio pattern that, rhythmically, is very similar to the triplet/gallop that you learned in Example 6-2. The only real difference is the way the part is written.

Section D (Repeat Verse)

Section E (Repeat Chorus)

Section F (Bridge 1): The first part of the bridge stays in the 3/4 meter of the chorus but switches to a straight gallop. By utilizing the B string, bridge 1 also steps slightly outside of the eighties vibe that the rest of the song creates (in general, five-string basses and low-tuning were not very common in the eighties). This part uses the B harmonic minor scale.

Section G (Bridge 2): The second part of the bridge returns to a 4/4 meter and uses eighth notes, mixed with a few sixteenth notes, to create a driving rhythm. Rather than using one of the scales that we've learned, this riff features chromatic movement. The A-string notes in this riff move up a minor 3rd, from E to G, and then down to F♯ and F♮ before returning to E.

Section H (Intro Reprise): A shortened version of the intro to the song.

Section I (Repeat Verse)

Section J (Repeat Chorus)

Section K (End of Song): A final, accented E note ends the song powerfully.

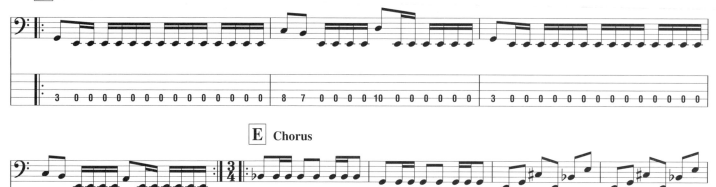

D Verse

E Chorus

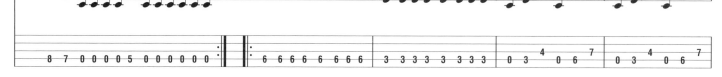

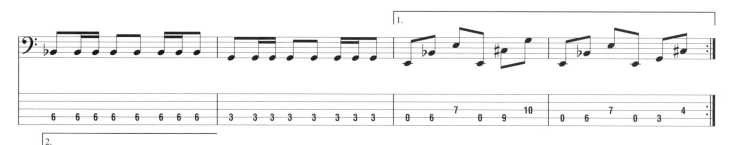

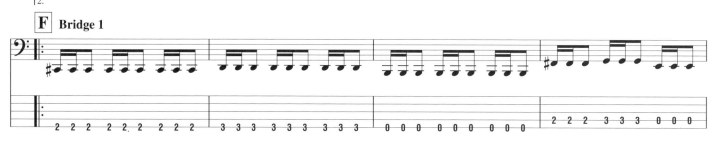

F Bridge 1

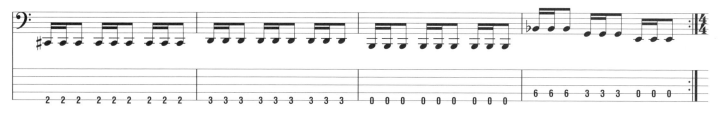

G Bridge 2

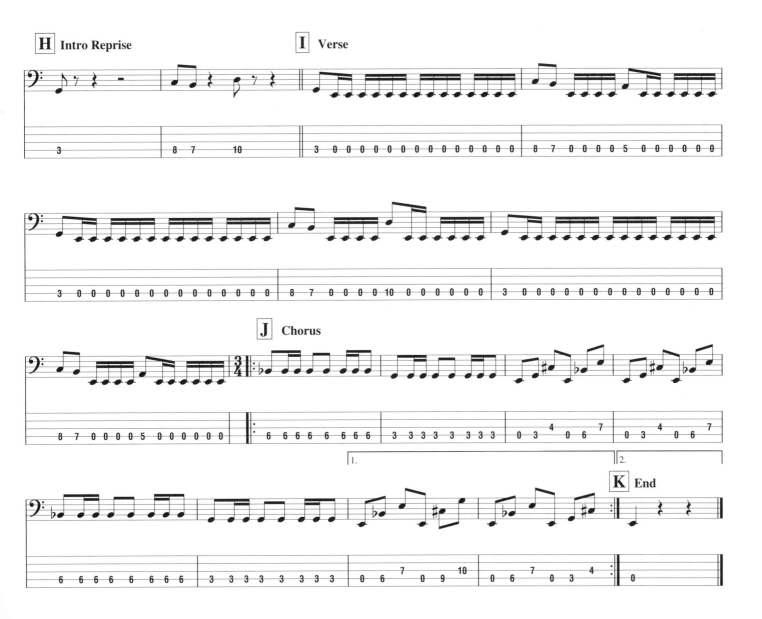

SONG EXAMPLE 2

This song features a combination of triplet grooves and syncopated modern metal riffing.

Song Structure and Performance Notes

Section A (Verse): This riff features a typical modern metal rhythm pattern. The riff is so focused on rhythm that it stays on a single note for its duration.

Section B (Chorus): Here, the riffing switches to a diminished scale/triplet-groove pattern. The arpeggio sections feature position shifts that might seem daunting, but they should come quite naturally if you incorporate the notated slides. The triplet/gallop note grouping also makes an appearance in this riff.

Section C (Extended Chorus): After repeating the verse and playing the chorus, you'll play the chorus again. This extension of the chorus is a tried-and-true technique of building anticipation for the song's bridge.

Section D (Bridge 1): This section features another syncopated modern metal riff. This riff, however, uses polymeter (see Examples 5-10 and 5-11). The guitar, bass, and kick drums all play this 3/4 rhythm:

Meanwhile, the drummer's hands (snare and cymbals) give the riff a decidedly 4/4 feel. The end result is that, for every three measures of 4/4, the guitar, bass, and kick drums will play the aforementioned pattern four times. The math behind this songwriting technique is really quite simple, but it can add a lot of interest to a riff by creating the illusion of complexity.

Section E (Bridge 1 Extended): This is the same riff as the one found in the previous section, but now the drums have created a double-time feel on the snare to build tension. Despite this change, the same 4/4 | 3/4 polymeter applies.

Section F (Bridge 2): For the second part of the bridge, the riffing switches back to a triplet feel. This time, the scale used is G harmonic minor. While the guitar-riffing features octave chords and speed picking, the bass plays a melodic eighth-note triplet line using additional notes from the scale.

Section G (Repeat Bridge 1)

Section H (Repeat Bridge 1 Extension)

Section I (Transition): This part uses a simple technique to segue between the bridge and the tag at the end of the song. Moving up a half step from the bridge's syncopated C♯ vamp to D and then down a minor 3rd to B sets up a smooth transition to the diminished arpeggio lick in the tag.

Section J (Tag): The song ends with an extended version of the diminished arpeggio licks from the chorus riff. Once again, a final accented note (this time an open B) gives the song a strong ending.

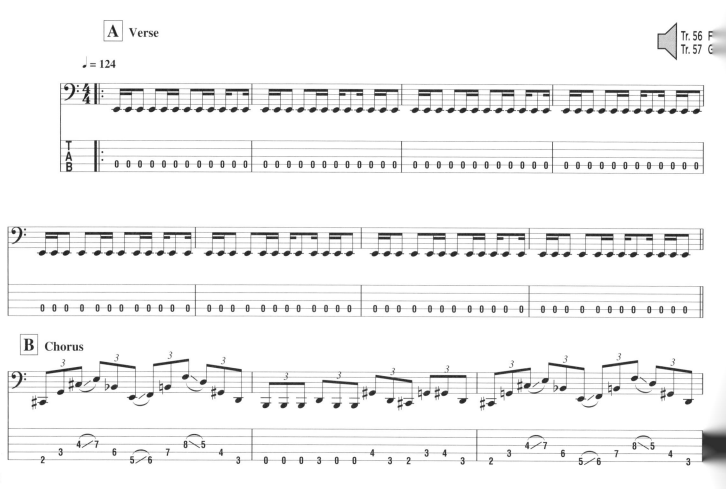

SONG EXAMPLE 3

OK, just in case you thought you were going to get through this whole book without playing along to some serious high-speed thrash beats and blasting, this song is here to prove you wrong. This sort of intense death/thrash metal is one of my favorite varieties of extreme metal. If you've been practicing the other songs in this chapter, you're probably good and warmed up by now—and that's a good thing, because you'll need to be for this one!

Song Structure and Performance Notes

Section A (Intro): The song starts with "stabs" played by the drums and guitar, while the bass plays a repetitive four-note diminished pattern.

Section B (Verse 1): Expanding upon the idea that was introduced by the bass in the intro, the guitar and bass play an eighth-note E whole/half diminished scale pattern in unison while the drummer plays a fast thrash beat.

Section C (Transition): This section uses a simple two-chord transition in a way that is very similar to the transition in Song Example 2. After the two chords are played, there are two stabs before the song launches into the second half of the verse. Transitions such as these are common throughout the song, so to avoid redundancy, I won't bother including the rest of them in this outline.

Section D (Verse 2): The second half of the verse takes the riff down a perfect 4th, to the B whole/half diminished scale, and the eighth-note guitar/bass unison assault continues; this time, with a furious bomb-blast beat being played by the drummer to ramp up the intensity.

Section E (Chorus): The chorus keeps the eighth notes pumping relentlessly, using the E half/whole diminished scale rather than the whole/half diminished of the verse. The drums switch to an eighth-note double-bass pattern, further accentuating the groove. When you play repeat ending #1 of this section, try playing the last two notes (C♯ and D) on either the ninth and tenth frets of the E string or the fourth and fifth frets of the A string. Both ways of playing it are fine; just pick the one that you think sounds and feels best.

Section F (Bridge 1): After repeating sections B, D, and E, the song enters the first section of the bridge. In the first half of bridge 1, there's a brief respite from the nearly constant stream of eighth notes that you've been playing thus far, as the bass follows the kick and snare of the more open drum beat being played in those measures (see Examples 7-2 through 7-4 for more bass lines of this type). For the second half of bridge 1, the eighth-note pulse is back as you join the guitar to play a busy C♯ Hungarian minor lick.

Section G (Bridge 2): The second bridge section uses the Hungarian minor scale again—this time, F♯ rather than C♯. While the guitars tremolo-pick the melody, the bass alternates between playing a quarter-note unison line and an eighth-note line. This part also features an odd meter (5/4). Odd meters can be intimidating at first, but they really shouldn't be. You're already familiar with meters of three beats, like 3/4, and meters with four beats, like 4/4, so a measure with five beats (in this case, 5/4) should be no problem for you to follow.

Section H (Intro Reprise): This time, the intro features the bass playing a vamp based on verse 2 rather than verse 1, as was the case in the first intro.

Section I (Repeat Verse 2)

Section J (Repeat Chorus)

Section K (End of Song): The song ends with the notes A♯/B♭, G, and E, which outline the E diminished arpeggio and reinforce the overall diminished tonality of the song.

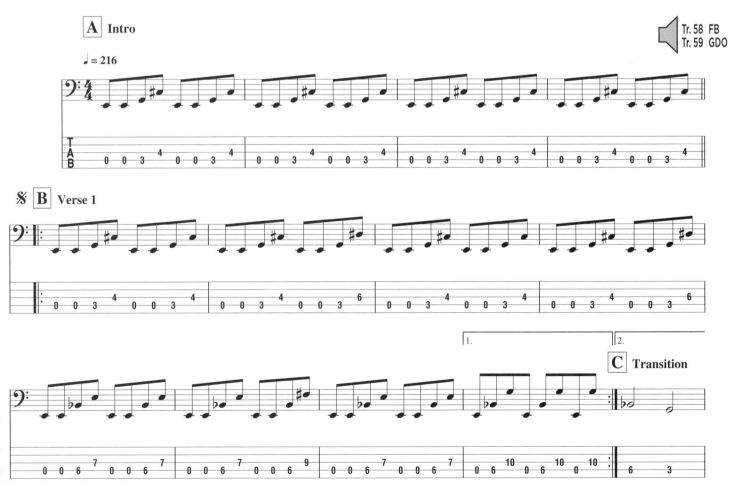

CONCLUSION

Now that you've worked through the exercises in this book, you should be much better prepared to play in an extreme metal band. Your chops have probably improved a lot along the way, but beyond that, you should have developed a better sense of how to create a bass line that is powerful, interesting, and complements your band's music. Chops and speed are important, but you don't have to be a fast bassist to be a great bassist and to write great bass lines. Practice hard, be a team player, and do your best to make your band sound as heavy as possible—that's what extreme metal bass is all about.

TRACK LIST

Track	Description
1	Tuning Notes
2	Example 5-1 full band
3	Example 5-1 guitar and drums only
4	Example 5-2 full band
5	Example 5-2 guitar and drums only
6	Example 5-3 full band
7	Example 5-3 guitar and drums only
8	Example 5-4 full band
9	Example 5-4 guitar and drums only
10	Example 5-5 full band
11	Example 5-5 guitar and drums only
12	Example 5-6 full band
13	Example 5-6 guitar and drums only
14	Example 5-7 full band
15	Example 5-7 guitar and drums only
16	Example 5-8 full band
17	Example 5-8 guitar and drums only
18	Example 5-9 full band
19	Example 5-9 guitar and drums only
20	Example 5-10 full band
21	Example 5-10 guitar and drums only
22	Example 5-11 full band
23	Example 5-11 guitar and drums only
24	Example 6-1 full band
25	Example 6-1 guitar and drums only
26	Example 6-2 full band
27	Example 6-2 guitar and drums only
28	Example 6-3 full band
29	Example 6-3 guitar and drums only
30	Example 7-1 full band
31	Example 7-1 guitar and drums only
32	Example 7-2 full band
33	Example 7-2 guitar and drums only
34	Example 7-3 full band
35	Example 7-3 guitar and drums only

RECORDING CREDITS

Drum programming and bass: **Alex Webster**
Guitar: **Ron Jarzombek**

Bass recorded at **Hell Whole Studios**
Guitar recorded at **Live Oak Studios**
Mixed and mastered by **Erik Rutan**, at **Mana Studios**

ACKNOWLEDGMENTS

Special thanks to my wife, Alison. Also, thanks to Erik Rutan, Ron Jarzombek, Brian Elliott, Joel McIver, Paul Conroy, Chuck Andrews, S.G. "Scooter" Davis, and everyone at Hal Leonard.

Alex Webster uses Spector basses, DR strings, SWR amplifiers, EMG pickups, Radial DI boxes, Line 6 amp modelers, Monster Cables, and Planet Waves straps.

ABOUT THE AUTHOR

Alex Webster is the bassist and a founding member of the death metal band Cannibal Corpse. Throughout their 20-plus-year career he has been their only bass player and has performed on all of their recordings and releases, including 11 studio albums, a live album, two EPs, and several DVDs. He has also toured extensively with Cannibal Corpse, having performed in over 50 countries on five continents.

In addition to his work with Cannibal Corpse, Alex is also part of the instrumental extreme metal band Blotted Science, whose 2007 album *The Machinations of Dementia* received wide critical acclaim. He has also made occasional guest appearances on other extreme metal recordings, most notably on Hate Eternal's recent album *Fury and Flames*.

A native of the Buffalo area, Alex currently resides in Florida with his wife Alison and their dogs.

BASS NOTATION LEGEND

Bass music can be notated two different ways: on a *musical staff*, and in *tablature*.

THE MUSICAL STAFF shows pitches and rhythms and is divided by bar lines into measures. Pitches are named after the first seven letters of the alphabet.

TABLATURE graphically represents the bass fingerboard. Each horizontal line represents a string, and each number represents a fret.

3rd string, open   2nd string, 2nd fret   1st & 2nd strings open, played together

HAMMER-ON: Strike the first (lower) note with one finger, then sound the higher note (on the same string) with another finger by fretting it without picking.

PULL-OFF: Place both fingers on the notes to be sounded. Strike the first note and without picking, pull the finger off to sound the second (lower) note.

LEGATO SLIDE: Strike the first note and then slide the same fret-hand finger up or down to the second note. The second note is not struck.

SHIFT SLIDE: Same as legato slide, except the second note is struck.

TRILL: Very rapidly alternate between the notes indicated by continuously hammering on and pulling off.

TREMOLO PICKING: The note is picked as rapidly and continuously as possible.

VIBRATO: The string is vibrated by rapidly bending and releasing the note with the fretting hand.

SHAKE: Using one finger, rapidly alternate between two notes on one string by sliding either a half-step above or below.

NATURAL HARMONIC: Strike the note while the fret hand lightly touches the string directly over the fret indicated.

MUFFLED STRINGS: A percussive sound is produced by laying the fret hand across the string(s) without depressing them and striking them with the pick hand.

BEND: Strike the note and bend up the interval shown.

BEND AND RELEASE: Strike the note and bend up as indicated, then release back to the original note. Only the first note is struck.

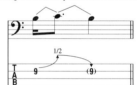

RIGHT-HAND TAP: Hammer ("tap") the fret indicated with the "pick-hand" index or middle finger and pull off to the note fretted by the fret hand.

LEFT-HAND TAP: Hammer ("tap") the fret indicated with the "fret-hand" index or middle finger.

SLAP: Strike ("slap") string with right-hand thumb.

POP: Snap ("pop") string with right-hand index or middle finger.

Additional Musical Definitions

>	*(accent)*	• Accentuate note (play it louder).
^	*(accent)*	• Accentuate note with great intensity.
•	*(staccato)*	• Play the note short.
⊓		• Downstroke
∨		• Upstroke
D.S. al Coda		• Go back to the sign (%), then play until the measure marked "*To Coda*," then skip to the section labelled "*Coda*."

D.C. al Fine	• Go back to the beginning of the song and play until the measure marked "***Fine***" (end).
Bass Fig.	• Label used to recall a recurring pattern.
Fill	• Label used to identify a brief melodic figure which is to be inserted into the arrangement.
tacet	• Instrument is silent (drops out).
	• Repeat measures between signs.
1. 2.	• When a repeated section has different endings, play the first ending only the first time and the second ending only the second time.

NOTE: Tablature numbers in parentheses mean:
1. The note is being sustained over a system (note in standard notation is tied), or
2. The note is sustained, but a new articulation (such as a hammer-on, pull-off, slide or vibrato) begins.